Momma

Tazia Kellogg

BookLeaf
Publishing

Presentation by *BookLeaf Publishing*

Web: www.bookleafpub.com

E-mail: info@bookleafpub.com

ISBN: 978-93-95088-23-7

First edition 2022

Sunday Morning

The boy is up like the sun

Immediately nagging for chips, chips for breakfast

A rainbow of berries instead, Contented by the offer
of pancakes
A whipped cream topping, of course

Sunday Afternoon

The sun is high in the sky

The day is flying by, as fast as we can flip through
the pages of his favorite books

As fast as El Toro Loco tears down the rainbow
mansions
        He builds and rebuilds

Grilled cheese for lunch with tomatoes

And chips and gummy bears and grapes

All the day's toys stay scattered on the floor,
silently napping
        Mom, boy, pup, and kitten asleep

Sunday Night

Mom is winding down with the sun

Cleaning up alone, dinner alone, sitting with the pup

Way too much time spent staring at a phone
　　　Mom misses her boy when he's gone

Work Day

Warm yellow light peaks through the blinds, stripes
the walls, opens eyes

Blue light clock glows with the time

The woman turns, determined to sleep
          Realistically, wistfully just a few minutes,
wishfully so many more

Minutes to rise, minutes to dress, minutes to brush,
walk, eat, and shut the door behind her

First to work, the time clock chirps

The days feel long, the work's dull
         Eight hours daydreaming of anything else

Trivia Night

5

Thursday nights after the sun goes down

Five purple hazes for the table

The questions are tough, our gears are spinning
    Guessing them right and knowing them wrong

Trouble at Daycare

Momma and Dad both called for a meeting at day's
end

Detailing that the boy has been misbehaving

Throwing toys, screaming, and pushing and hitting
    It sounds really bad

They're sending board game dollars to daycare

Teaching consequences and rewards, for his
behaviors of choice

A responsibility chart on the fridge
    Stars mark more bad days than good

Birthday Party

Mid-afternoon on a beautiful day, the boy's invited to eat and to play

Kids in the backyard, running willy-nilly, they never realize they look a little silly

Worried about keeping hands and feet to himself, not worried at all, he's behaving well
Happy First Birthday, dear friend

Gardening on the Balcony

Basil and oregano need the sun, to thrive, to grow

Rosemary and thyme need water, but not too much

No holes in the box, no place for too much water to
go
       The rain flooded the box, time and time
again

Momma loves the plants, like a pup or a pet

Holes hammered into the sides of the box and the
bottom

Excess water removed by hand
       Hands dirty but the herbs thrive

Sprained Ankle

A playoff game, a change from the usual
lackadaisical play

Bodies collide, twisted knees, twisted ankles

Pain when she walks and pain when she sits, the
ankle is wrong
        They did not even win

Every Other Wednesday Night

Home before sunset, able to watch the colors change

Miles long walks, an hour long shower, easy to make dinner

Momma puts on a movie to lull her to sleep
        The pup keeps her company when the boy is away

Every Other Wednesday Night

When the sun's still out after daycare and work and it
they're only night this week

Requests for throwing rocks in the river, walks down
the street, trips to the playground and over and over
again, something to eat

The favorites are spaghetti and meatballs or chicken
tenders
Anything really if it is covered in cheese

Crocheting

She cries about money she doesn't have

She thinks about quitting

The yarn in the closet, every color, every style
        Momma quits crying and begins crocheting

A skill, a coping mechanism, she learned it later in life

Mind clearing patterns, intentional stitches, calming movements

Through the loop, over the hook, pull
        A blanket to soothe, tomorrow Momma will try again

Flat Tire

No sun this morning, it's snowing quite hard on the
way to visit a friend

A whole chunk missing from the front passenger side
tire

Momma pulls over, pulls out her spare donut, pulls
out the kit
          She thinks she can swap it herself

Before the spare tire is out of the trunk, before
Momma attempts by herself

Passcrsby pull up behind to help

The man is so kind, Momma appreciates the help
          She knows next time she can swap it herself

Walking the Dog

She doesn't seem to notice the sun; she gets up with
Momma and she goes down with the boy when he's
there

The harness means a long walk, not just out to pee

She has enough energy to walk forever, catch every
squirrel, rabbit, and deer
       Pulling forward and sideways at whatever
catches her eye

Momma enjoys these walks to, admires nature,
absorbs the heat from the sun

Snapping turtles, deer, black squirrels, white and gray
squirrels and wildflowers all around

Running and walking, passing mile markers, passing
hours
       Walks with the pup are pure happiness

Hatching Chicks

Started with a carton of eggs during a trip to the
grocer

Questions about breaking, questions about hatching,
questions about chicks and chickens

Then they got an incubator, then they got some fertile
eggs
        21 days to hatch baby chickens

Rainy Day

Clouds, gray and heavy, cover the sun

Next to the river too much rain is a problem

Momma sits outside to watch the drops fall, wrapped
in a blanket watching for lightning to strike and
thunder to sound
       Just please don't flood again

Friday Night

Thank God It's Friday

Work done, time to go home, time to have fun

Maybe bowling, a movie, some time with best friends
         If not for fun, for relaxation, Momma's long
week is done

No Work Day

The forecast says sunny, about 60some degrees

Momma is not going to work today

Visiting a field of tulips, red and white and purple
and orange
        Time well spent with friends

The table she chooses is in the light on one side

Gluten free chicken tenders and fries

The conversation is hilarious, serious, and familiar
       Time flies by, fruit flies like bananas

Sunday Morning

Ignoring the sun, Momma stays in bed past 8AM

It is the only day of the week that she can

Unless she has somewhere to be, soccer, or breakfast
with her family
        Snuggled up so warm with her pup

Sunday Afternoon

In the streaks of light from the window, dust and hair
can be seen

"Sunday is cleaning day," She hears her own mother
say

She starts in the kitchen, dishes and wiping down the
stove
        Waters the plants, satisfied with the new
growth

Momma receives her boy, warmth from the sky
above and her heart

Hugs and kisses and games and movies

The boy is excited to be back with Momma, Momma
missed the boy so much
        Today he can have ~basically~ anything he
wants

Sunday Night

They can't see the sun from the bathroom

Bubbles and trucks floating around the tub

Warm jammies straight from the dryer
       Love and blankets and hugs and kisses all
getting tucked in together tonight